FIGURE SKATING
Champions

Steve Milton & Gérard Châtaigneau

Firefly Books

A FIREFLY BOOK

Published by Firefly Books Ltd., 2002

First Printing

National Library of Canada Cataloguing in Publication Data

Milton, Steve
    Figure skating champions / Steve Milton ; photographs by Gérard Châtaigneau.

ISBN 1-55297-658-0

    1. Skaters—Biography—Juvenile literature. 2. Skating—Juvenile literature. I. Châtaigneau, Gérard II. Title.

GV850.A2M53 2002   j796.91'2'0922   C2002-901742-4

Publisher Cataloging-in-Publication Data (U.S.)

Milton, Steve.
    Figure skating champions / Steve Milton ; photographs by Gérard Châtaigneau.—
1st ed.
[32] p. : ill. , col. photos. ; cm.
Summary: Profiles of 23 famous skaters from World and Olympic Championships.
Illustrated with color photographs.
ISBN 1-55297-658-0 (pbk.)
1. Skaters—Biography—Juvenile literature. 2. Skating—Juvenile literature.
(1. Skaters—Biography. 2. Skating.) I. Châtaigneau, Gérard. II. Title.
  796.91/2/0922 B 21   CIP   GV850.A2.M55 2002

Published in Canada in 2002 by
Firefly Books Ltd.
3680 Victoria Park Avenue
Toronto, Ontario M2H 3K1

Published in the United States in 2002 by
Firefly Books (U.S.) Inc.
P.O. Box 1338, Ellicott Station
Buffalo, New York 14205

Cover and interior design by Christine Gilham
Printed and bound in Canada by
Friesens, Altona, Manitoba

The Publisher acknowledges the financial support of the Government of Canada through the Book Publishing Industry Development Program for its publishing activities.

The Heart of a Champion

No matter what the sport, you can always recognize the champions. They carry themselves with pride. They learned to work incredibly hard, usually at a very young age. They know how to overcome difficulties and doubt. They are willing to make great sacrifices to become the best at what they do.

And no matter what the sport, the heart of its champion is always the same: brave, determined and strong; willing to ignore pain, injury and fatigue. The young men and women in this book are all champions: of their country, of their continent, of the Olympics or of the world.

The 19th Winter Olympics in Salt Lake City saw the world's best skaters at their physical and emotional peaks. New stars were created, and they will make skating news for years to come. Reigning champions were applauded and appreciated for what they have done and will still do. Older legends were celebrated and thanked for the wonderful careers they have given us.

One of the many beautiful aspects of figure skating is that its champions never really retire. The Olympics, for instance, highlighted the final season in the long and brilliant amateur careers of Elvis Stojko, Todd Eldredge, Marina Anissina and Gwendal Peizerat. But they will take their brilliance into professional skating, and we will see them on tour.

Those who remain in Olympic-eligible figure skating will continue to amaze us with their artistry and physical skills. But they will always be challenged by newer, and younger, athletes – just as they were once the newer, younger athletes who challenged those before them.

Figure skating is deep in talent, and that's what creates exciting competition. Every year, the skill level seems to improve. Pairs teams Jamie Salé and David Pelletier and Elena Berezhnaya and Anton Sikharulidze have redefined the event.

The dance teams, inspired by Marina Anissina and Gwendal Peizerat, tell better and more intricate stories than ever before.

The women's division is pushing the technical envelope. Sarah Hughes, Irina Slutskaya and Sasha Cohen are doing innovative jumps and combinations, while trying to reach the artistry of Michelle Kwan.

And the men raise the bar higher every year. Alexei Yagudin and Evgeny Plushenko perform extraordinarily demanding combination jumps, but their sense of performance makes it all look easy. Almost every season, Tim Goebel seems to set a new quad record.

In short, it's becoming more and more difficult to be a figure skating champion. So it's more and more important to have the heart of a champion.

Everyone in this book has one.

Contents

Sarah Hughes

BORN	May 2, 1985, Great Neck, New York
HOMETOWN	Great Neck, New York
COACH	Robin Wagner

QUICK FACTS:

- Sarah always wears her lucky Peggy Fleming T-shirt before she skates.

- "I often go out and am so worried about whether I'm going to skate fast, or spin well," Sarah said after her Olympic performance. "But this time, I wanted just to have fun with it."

- When she has time, Sarah enjoys playing the violin. She wants to study medicine.

By following her own advice, Sarah Hughes became an Olympic champion.

"You can't be safe. You have to tell everyone you want it," Sarah once said. "You've got to grab for it." Sarah did grab for it by presenting the most difficult program in women's skating history at the 2002 Olympics. She became the first woman to land two triple-triple combinations in the same performance, which was enough to beat Michelle Kwan and Irina Slutskaya for the Olympic gold medal. And she was just 16 years old!

But Sarah has always been ahead of her time.

When Sarah was three, she got tired of waiting for her mother to finish tying her brothers' and sisters' laces each time the family went skating. So Sarah learned to tie her own laces, and she got on the ice sooner.

When she was six, Sarah skated in front of large audiences at arenas in New York. And when she was eight, she toured France and Switzerland with some of the most famous skaters in the world. By the time she was 12, Sarah could do all five triple jumps that the world's best female skaters were landing. That helped her win the U.S. junior championship. She was competing at the senior World championships when she was 13, winning a bronze medal when she was 15.

All her hard work paid off at the Salt Lake City Olympics. Michelle and Irina were favored to battle it out for the gold. When Sarah finished fourth in the short program, most people thought she might not even win a medal. And no one thought she could win the gold.

But just before the Olympics, Sarah and her coach, Robin Wagner, had improved Sarah's freeskate program, changing the last 90 seconds of music and adding a second triple-triple combination. Sarah was telling everyone she wanted it.

She skated brilliantly, and when she finished she received a roaring standing ovation. Then she had to wait until four more skaters performed before she found out that she was the new Olympic champion.

It was well worth the wait.

Achievements: Olympic champion, 2002; World bronze medalist, 2001; bronze medalist, Grand Prix Final 2001, 2002; silver medalist, U.S. Nationals 2001; bronze medalist, U.S. Nationals 1999, 2002.

Michelle Kwan

BORN	July 7, 1980, Torrance, California
HOMETOWN	Lake Arrowhead, California
COACH	Herself

QUICK FACTS:

- Michelle's parents moved from Hong Kong to California, where they opened a restaurant. Michelle began skating when she was five, after watching her older brother play hockey. She won her first competition when she was seven.

- In 2000, *People* magazine chose Michelle as one of the "50 Most Beautiful People in the World."

- Michelle always skates wearing the Chinese good luck charm given to her by her grandmother.

Michelle Kwan might not have captured an Olympic championship, but she is the best female skater of her era.

"It just wasn't meant to be," Michelle said after she finished third at the 2002 Olympics in Salt Lake City. She won the silver medal at the 1998 Olympics in Nagano, Japan. The judging vote was very close for that gold medal, won by Tara Lipinski, and her graciousness in accepting the decision won Michelle millions of new fans.

She already had millions of fans. They had been following her career since she burst into the spotlight in 1994, when she was a 13-year-old alternate on the U.S. Olympic team that also included Nancy Kerrigan and Tonya Harding.

She was just 15 when she won her first World championship in 1996, and was champion again in 1998, 2000 and 2001. In the years she didn't win, she finished second. In addition to winning medals at seven consecutive World championships, Michelle holds six U.S. skating titles.

Now that's consistency!

After the 1998 Games, Michelle kept competing, partly for the chance at another Olympic medal in 2002. "But it wasn't just that," she explained. "It's being on the ice every day – falling down, getting back up and enjoying skating. Athletes say they want to get into the 'zone,' and that's what I'm striving for."

She got into that zone in 2002, when she scored her 27th perfect 6.0 mark at U.S. Nationals, the most ever.

Just four months before the 2002 Olympics, Michelle split from coach Frank Carroll, who had been teaching her for nearly 10 years. Her father Danny was there for moral support, but Michelle was essentially coaching herself.

Michelle's gracefulness, choreography and light touch on the ice have made her one of the most popular skaters in history. But she has a full life outside of skating. She attends college, has written two books, visits children's hospitals and serves as a spokesperson for the Children's Miracle Network.

As Michelle so rightly says, "the gold medal would not complete me as a person."

Achievements: World champion, 1996, 1998, 2000, 2001; World silver medalist, 1997, 1999, 2002; Olympic silver medalist, 1998; Olympic bronze medalist, 2002; Grand Prix Final champion, 1996; Grand Prix Final silver medalist, 2000, 2001; six-time U.S. champion.

Sasha Cohen

BORN	October 26, 1984, Westwood, California
HOMETOWN	Laguna Niguel, California
COACH	John Nicks

QUICK FACTS:

■ During the opening ceremonies at the 2002 Winter Olympics, President Bush spoke to Sasha's mom on Sasha's cell phone.

■ Sasha has designed some of her practice dresses with the help of her mother and costume designer Mark Talbott. One of her long-term goals is to be a fashion designer.

■ Sasha most admires Scott Hamilton and Kurt Browning, who won eight World titles between them. Kurt did the world's first quad, and Sasha is trying to become the first woman to do one.

At four feet 11 inches, Sasha Cohen was one of the smallest athletes at the 2002 Winter Olympics. But she made one of the biggest impacts.

She came to Salt Lake City to face the planet's best skaters without having the important experience of competing at a World championship. Yet Sasha finished third in the short program and fourth overall. It was an impressive debut at the sport's highest level. Of course, Sasha is used to making an impression.

She began her athletic career as a gymnast, winning several competitions before switching to figure skating when she was seven years old. Today, she is among the most flexible skaters in the world, and she rotates easily in her jumps and spins.

That's why most people think Sasha will be the first woman in skating history to land a quadruple jump in competition. The fact that she is going for the quadruple, when most women aren't even practicing one, shows just how feisty Sasha is.

When many of her current opponents were competing at the 1998 Olympics, Sasha was still a novice skater. But she started her rapid rise into skating's elite the next season, when she finished second at U.S. junior Nationals. A year later she made a splashy entrance into the senior ranks, finishing second at the 2000 U.S. Nationals after winning the short program.

Skating fans were mesmerized by her quick turns in the air and her amazing spiral – a trademark move in which she glides around the ice in complete control, with one leg extended almost straight up in the air above her head.

Sasha decided not to attempt the quad at either the 2002 Nationals or Salt Lake Olympics, because there was so much at stake.

"My goal was for her to make the Olympic team," her coach, John Nicks, explains. "But," he adds, "I see no reason why ladies can't continue to progress in technical content."

And Sasha could not agree more.

Achievements: 4th, Winter Olympics 2002; 4th, World championships, 2002; 3rd, Trophée Lalique 2001; silver medalist, U.S. Nationals 2000, 2002; 6th, World junior championships 2000.

Jennifer Robinson

BORN	December 2, 1976, Goderich, Ontario
HOMETOWN	Windsor, Ontario
COACH	Michelle Leigh

QUICK FACTS:

- Jennifer's brother Jason plays professional hockey. Her uncle, Gaston Gingras, won a Stanley Cup with the NHL's Montreal Canadiens.

- Jennifer is involved with a number of charities, including Tim Horton's Camp Day, the Alzheimer's Society, and the Heart and Stroke Foundation.

Other people might have stopped believing in her, but Jennifer Robinson never lost faith in herself.

And so the graceful skater from Windsor, Ontario, rebounded from a 15th-place showing at the 2001 World championships to deliver the best season of her long career. In 2001–02, Jennifer skated personal-best programs in two Grand Prix events, won her fifth National championship, and qualified for her first Olympics. At Salt Lake City, she skated an error-free short program. She was confident and aggressive in the freeskate and finished seventh overall, much higher than anyone had predicted for her.

Jennifer performed her Olympic freeskate just after watching Canada's women's hockey team win their gold medal. For her, the "coolest thing" about her Olympic experience was that Brian Orser was in the stands, "watching me have my Olympic moment." Brian, who won two Olympic silver medals, trained at the Mariposa Club, where Jennifer has trained since she was 15 years old.

You could call Jennifer a late bloomer, because in a skating world dominated by teenagers, she has enjoyed her greatest successes while in her twenties. She has always been an elegant skater with excellent body lines. But Jennifer also struggled with confidence on the ice. She would skate cautiously, worried about landing her jumps.

Jennifer is used to fighting back from disappointment. After winning the Canadian junior title in 1994 and finishing second at Nationals in 1995, she won her first senior championship in 1996. But then came two years of disheartening third-place finishes, when she failed to qualify for the World championships. Since then, though, she's won four straight Canadian titles, the first woman to do that in 25 years. Twice she finished in the World's top 10.

For much of her championship reign, she has had to answer questions about why Canadian women haven't fared well at the international level. She handles those difficult questions with honesty and wit.

And along with her famous sense of humor, she has developed self-confidence on the ice.

Achievements: 7th, Winter Olympics 2002; 8th, World championships 2000; 9th, World championships 2002; bronze medalist, Skate Canada 1999; five-time Canadian champion.

Irina Slutskaya

BORN	February 9, 1979, Moscow
HOMETOWN	Moscow
COACH	Zhanna Gromova

If energy had a face, it would look like Irina Slutskaya.

For years, the dynamo from Moscow has been one of the most lively skaters on the world scene, forcing her competitors to become more daring and athletic. When she was young, her grandmother nicknamed her the "typhoon." And Irina has continued to storm her way through the skating ranks.

In her earliest competitions, winners got flowers or dolls. "But," says Irina, "I was always crying, 'I want a medal!'"

Irina won the shiniest medal of all at Nagano, Japan, in March 2002, when she became just the second Russian woman to win the World championship.

"A couple of times I was just so close I wondered if it would ever happen," Irina says. "And now that it's finally come, I'm just so happy."

Irina was World junior champion at 16. At 17, she became the first Russian woman to win the European championship. She went on to become the first woman to land a triple Salchow–triple toe loop combination, the first to do a triple Lutz–triple loop, and also the first to do a triple-triple-double combination.

Because she was known mostly for the fierce athleticism of her skating, Irina worked very hard at becoming a more all-round skater. Her Biellmann spin (one leg pulled up over the head) is one of skating's most attractive moves, and she does it first on one foot, and then on the other.

Irina is the only woman to win three Grand Prix Finals. She has also won three silver medals at Worlds, and was silver medalist at the 2002 Olympics. She has more World medals than any other woman singles skater in Russian history.

She and Michelle Kwan have waged some memorable head-to-head battles. The two are longtime friends, but the feisty Irina says, "sometimes you have war on the ice." And she brings a lot of energy to that war.

Achievements: World champion, 2002; Olympic silver medalist, 2002; World silver medalist, 1999, 2000, 2001; Grand Prix Final champion, 2000, 2001, 2002; European champion, 1996, 1997, 2000, 2001.

Alexei Yagudin

BORN	March 18, 1980, Leningrad (St. Petersburg), Russia
HOMETOWN	St. Petersburg, Russia
COACH	Tatiana Tarasova

QUICK FACTS:

■ Although Alexei won the Olympics and four World championships, he has never won the Russian National championship.

■ As soon as he could afford it, Alexei bought his mother and grandmother their own apartment in St. Petersburg. "Without them," he says, "I would be no one."

■ Alexei's dog Lawrence is named after his "Lawrence of Arabia" freeskating program of 1998, with which he won the World title.

As soon as the music ended, Alexei Yagudin's face was no longer an iron mask. He grinned, punched his fist into the air and then kneeled down to kiss the ice.

He knew his performance to the movie theme "Man in the Iron Mask" was good enough to make him the 2002 Olympic champion. And he was right. He received four perfect 6.0s for presentation, and every other score was a 5.9. No other individual skater in Olympic history had received more than two 6.0s. A month later, he received more perfect marks when he won his fourth World title.

"I just held my knees and kissed the ice because I live in America," Alexei explains.

Alexei has bought a three-bedroom condominium in New Jersey. That home is an example of how far he's come from his childhood in Russia.

When Alexei's mother registered him for his first skating class at the age of four, "just to keep me busy," Russia was still under the communist system. His family was so poor that they had to share a small apartment with another family.

"It was a very tough time for me," Alexei recalls. "I was just skating, skating, skating." But all that skating paid off. At 18, he became the second-youngest World champion of all time.

Because he felt he wasn't getting enough attention from his coach, Alexei moved to the United States and began to take lessons from Tatiana Tarasova. "If I didn't go to America and Tatiana, I think I would have slid back and been just an average skater," Alexei says.

Alexei won the 1998, 1999 and 2000 World championships, but finished second to his rival, Evgeny Plushenko, at the 2001 Worlds. In that championship, he was skating with an injured foot and had to take several injections just to freeze the pain away.

"I wanted to prove that I'm a fighter and a good skater," he says.

He's much more than good. He's one of the best skaters in history, and he's an Olympic champion.

Achievements: Olympic champion, 2002; World champion, 1998, 1999, 2000, 2002; World silver medalist, 2001; Grand Prix Final champion, 1999, 2002; 5th, Winter Olympics 1998; European champion, 1999, 2000, 2002.

Timothy Goebel

BORN	September 10, 1980, Evanston, Illinois
HOMETOWN	Rolling Meadows, Illinois
COACH	Frank Carroll

He is called the Quad King, and Tim Goebel wears his crown well.

At the 2002 Winter Olympics, Tim Goebel added another item to his long line of "firsts" when he became the first skater to land three quadruple jumps in the same Olympic program. That gave him the bronze medal behind Alexei Yagudin and Evgeny Plushenko. Many people thought he could have won the silver. At Worlds in Nagano, he did win the silver.

Tim started skating in a Chicago suburb when he was four years old. By the age of eight he knew he wanted to be a jumper. By the time Tim was 17, when he won the junior Grand Prix Final, he was the first person to do a quadruple Salchow in competition and the first American to do any type of quad.

Later, he would become the first skater from any country to do a quad Salchow combined with a triple jump, and the first skater to include three quads in a program.

When he was 10, Tim left home to train with coaches Glyn Watts and Carol Heiss-Jenkins near Cleveland, Ohio. Three years later he was U.S. novice champion, and two years after that he became the national junior champion.

He completed the triple crown with his first U.S. senior title in 2001. He also finished fourth in the world that year. By then he had moved to California to work with coach Frank Carroll. He won his first major Grand Prix event (Skate America 2000) and was no longer just a leaper.

Tim works with talented Canadian choreographer Lori Nichol, who has spent a lot of time helping him to understand how his skating relates to his accompanying music. Now Tim thinks as much about his presentation as his jumps.

"I want to improve my artistry so that it's even stronger than my technical," he says. "I'm a little bit ahead in the jumping now, and I always want to keep that edge."

He's kept that edge, and at Salt Lake it helped him become the first American man to win an Olympic figure skating medal in 10 years.

QUICK FACTS:

- A pair of boots normally lasts a top skater six months. Because he jumps so much in practice, Tim often goes through a pair in two weeks.

- Tim has attended Case Western University in Ohio and Loyola Marymount in California. He has said he would like to attend Harvard Medical School.

- Tim was on the honor roll at school from 1992 to 1999.

Achievements: Olympic bronze medalist, 2002; World silver medalist, 2002; 4th, World championships 2001; bronze medalist, Grand Prix Final 2002; silver medalist, World junior championships 1997; junior Grand Prix Final champion, 1998; two-time U.S. National champion.

Elvis Stojko

BORN	March 22, 1972, Newmarket, Ontario
HOMETOWN	Richmond Hill, Ontario
COACH	Uschi Keszler

QUICK FACTS:

- As Elvis was growing up, figure skating was just one sport at which he excelled. He also raced dirtbikes. When his skating career is over, he may switch to racing cars.

- Elvis did history's first quad-double combination at the 1991 World championships; and the first quad-triple at the 1997 Grand Prix Final. He landed his last quad-triple on the same ice (Hamilton, Ontario) as his first one.

- He received the Meritorious Service Cross from Canada's Governor-General for contribution to sport.

There can be no doubt about this: Elvis Stojko changed the way men figure skate.

During Elvis's time on the world stage, no man could win a major competition without skating a program that was consistent and athletic, that told some kind of a story, and that included successful quadruple jumps.

When he and his close friend Todd Eldredge went to their first World championship in 1990, the event still included compulsory figures. Those were the slow tracings of figure eights, from which "figure" skating got its name.

But Elvis was never about slow tracings. He is all about strong, powerful skating with booming jumps. And he is also about being faithful to what he believes in.

"One thing I'm proud of is that I did it my way," Elvis says. "A lot of people didn't like my style, and I feel like I've had to fight against the odds all my career. But I've been true to myself the whole time."

Elvis was the first person ever to do a quadruple jump combined with a double jump, and he was also the first to do a quad-triple combination. Now, a male skater can't win a World or an Olympic title without two quad combinations. And many skaters follow Elvis's example and use action-movie soundtracks for their music.

Elvis's father enrolled him in karate when Elvis was seven, and by 16 he had a black belt. Elvis has included many karate and kung-fu moves in his skating programs, and the mental discipline required for martial arts has influenced his skating philosophy.

In 1995, Elvis injured his ankle so badly he couldn't walk. But one month later he won the World championship. In 1998, he had a groin injury that would keep him out of skating for nearly a year – but not before he won an Olympic silver medal.

Elvis won his final Canadian title in 2002. At his farewell Olympics five weeks later, he landed two quads in the same program for the first time in his career.

He was saying goodbye to the amateur ranks the same way he said hello: with class and with big jumps.

He'll now skate in the professional ranks.

Achievements: World champion, 1994, 1995, 1997; World silver medalist, 1993, 2000; World bronze medalist, 1992; Olympic silver medalist, 1994, 1998; Grand Prix Final champion, 1997; eight-time Canadian champion.

Todd Eldredge

BORN	August 28, 1971, Chatham, Massachusetts
HOMETOWN	Chatham
COACH	Richard Callaghan

Todd Eldredge retired from eligible skating exactly the same way he competed in it: with dignity and style.

Two days after the men's freeskate at the 2002 Winter Olympics, Todd announced that he was turning professional. Fans will still see him on tour, but it won't be the same at the Nationals and World championships without the veteran from Cape Cod.

Todd first competed at Worlds in 1990, the same year as his friend and longtime rival Elvis Stojko. He had just become the youngest (18) U.S. men's champion in 24 years.

"Back then I was known as the guy who had the jumps and not the artistry," he laughs. "Now it's the other way around."

He may not have the quiver of quads that some of the younger skaters possess, but Todd's overall strength always left him on or near the podium. His programs are elegant, his triple jumps are clean and his spins are probably the best in the world. That all-round ability led him to six U.S. titles and six World championship medals.

After winning a bronze medal at the 1991 Worlds, Todd ran into four years of bad luck. He hurt his back in 1992, and two years later was terribly sick during Nationals and didn't make the Olympic team. He almost quit skating that season, but decided to stick with it.

It was a good decision, because in 1995 he won the U.S. championship again. Within a year, he won the World championship.

He won two more medals at Worlds, but finished a disappointing fourth at the 1998 Olympics and decided to take two years off from heavy competition. In the 2000–01 season he returned to the demanding eligible ranks, hoping to capture an Olympic medal at Salt Lake.

It was a remarkable comeback. He became the oldest skater (29) to land a quad for the first time in competition, won a bronze medal at the 2001 Worlds, and at age 30 won his final U.S. championship. And though he didn't win an Olympic medal in 2002, the experience was, in Todd's words, "definitely worth it."

QUICK FACTS:

- Todd has donated money to his hometown, where a baseball diamond has been named in his honor.
- Golf is Todd's other sport. He is by far the best golfer among all the world's top skaters.
- He dedicates many hours working with the Blind and Handicapped Skating Association.

Achievements: World champion, 1996; World silver medalist, 1995, 1997, 1998; World bronze medalist, 1991, 2001; 4th, Winter Olympics 1998; 6th, Winter Olympics 2002; World junior champion, 1988; six-time U.S. champion.

Michael Weiss

BORN	August 2, 1976, Washington, DC
HOMETOWN	Fairfax, Virginia
COACH	Audrey Weisiger

QUICK FACTS:

- Michael was named Father of the Year in 1999 by the National Fatherhood Initiative.

- Michael recovered from a stress fracture in his ankle to win the 2000 U.S. Nationals.

Michael Weiss was born to be an elite athlete.

His father competed in gymnastics at the 1964 Summer Olympics, his mother was a national gymnastics champion, one of his sisters won the world junior diving championship, and another sister won a silver medal at the U.S. junior figure skating Nationals.

In 1998, when Michael made his first Olympic team, the Winter Games were in Japan, where his father had competed in the Summer Games.

Michael took up skating when he was nine and also competed in diving and gymnastics. The balance and body control required for those sports proved valuable in figure skating as well. Michael won the U.S. junior championship when he was 16, then won the World junior championship the next year.

In 1997, he nearly became the first American to land a quadruple jump. It took several video replays to show that he had barely two-footed the landing. "I was an up-and-coming skater at the time and needed to try something well beyond what the other skaters were doing," Michael explains. "My skating is much more well-balanced than it was before. I have a higher artistic mark now."

He did land his first quad at the 1999 Worlds, and went on to win the bronze medal. He won the bronze in 2000 as well. Both seasons, he also captured the U.S. title.

Despite his arrival in the upper ranks, Michael kept attempting the quad Lutz, which no skater has yet landed. Even at the 2002 World championships, when a strong short program put him in contention for a medal, he made a good, but unsuccessful, try at the quad Lutz in the freeskate. He finished sixth overall, but showed the heart of an athlete.

Michael is married to his choreographer, Lisa Thornton-Weiss, and they have two children. With his family life and his degree in business marketing, Michael is one of the most well-rounded men in the skating world.

Achievements: World bronze medalist, 1999, 2000; 7th, Winter Olympics 1998, 2002; World junior champion, 1994; two-time U.S. champion.

Evgeny Plushenko

BORN	November 3, 1982, Solnechi, Russia
HOMETOWN	St. Petersburg, Russia
COACH	Alexei Mishin

Evgeny Plushenko has the power of a weight lifter and the flexibility of a gymnast. That's because his first coach was, indeed, a bodybuilder. And when Evgeny was very young, his mother made him do difficult stretching exercises.

Evgeny started skating when he was four years old, in the Russian industrial city of Volgograd. He landed his first triple jump by the time he was seven. But when he was 11, the rink was shut down. So Evgeny and his mother moved to St. Petersburg, where he could train with the famous coach, Alexei Mishin.

Within three years, Evgeny landed his first quadruple jump. Just ten days later, he did his first quad-triple.

Because they had so little money, Evgeny and his mother shared a small apartment with another family, and his coach paid most of the rent. Growing up with so little, Evgeny was motivated to become successful at skating.

He is not just an extraordinary jumper. Evgeny also brings a dramatic artistry to his skating. He is the only man doing the demanding Biellmann spin, in which he grabs his skate and hoists his leg over his head. "My mother used to make me do so many stretching exercises when I was very young," he remembers. "I didn't want to do them, but now I thank her."

His unique combination of skills paid off quickly. He was a World bronze medalist at 15, and when he was 18 he won the World championship. That same season, he became the first man in history to do a quadruple-triple-double combination. He is also the first one to do a different program in the qualifying and the freeskate rounds at Worlds.

He is a very determined athlete. "I really want to show the world what I can do," Evgeny once said. "I want to be World, European and Olympic champion."

At the 2002 Olympics, Evgeny really showed his strength, flexibility and determination. He rallied from a disappointing short program and went on to win the silver medal.

Achievements: World champion, 2001; Olympic silver medalist, 2002; World silver medalist, 1999; Grand Prix Final champion, 2000, 2001; World junior champion, 1997.

Jamie Salé & David Pelletier

BORN (Jamie)	April 21, 1977, Calgary
BORN (David)	November 22, 1974, Sayabec, Quebec
HOMETOWNS	Red Deer, Alberta; Sayabec, Quebec
COACH	Jan Ullmark

QUICK FACTS:

- David has a great sense of humor. When he and Jamie were awarded gold medals after originally being named silver medalists at the Olympics, he said, "We hope we get the bronze medal too, so we can have the entire collection."

- "The greatest thing about two people on ice is when they can move like one," says their choreographer Lori Nichol. "That's what Jamie and David can do."

- Jamie and David's gold was Canada's first Olympic figure skating gold since 1960.

It took four days for the right decision to be made, but Jamie Salé and David Pelletier finally were given the Olympic gold medals they deserved.

The expressive Canadian pair thought they had performed their "Love Story" freeskate perfectly at the 2002 Winter Olympics. So did the sold-out audience.

But when the marks were posted, the crowd booed because the three-time Canadian champions had finished second, on a 5–4 judges' split. A few days later it was discovered that the French judge had broken a rule, and her vote was not counted. So Jamie and David were awarded gold medals, as were original winners Elena Berezhnaya and Anton Sikharulidze.

"We never had anything against Anton and Elena. They skated a gold medal performance," David says. "We had something against the system."

Because they were so gracious in accepting what was clearly a wrong decision, the Canadian skaters became famous around the world.

Jamie started skating at the age of five in Red Deer, Alberta, and showed tremendous talent as a singles skater. She moved to Edmonton and became a pairs skater before going back to singles. She finished 12th at the 1994 Olympics with Jason Turner.

David, meanwhile, was growing up in the small Quebec town of Sayabec. He was a good swimmer and excelled at singles and pairs skating. He won the national novice and junior pairs titles with Julie Laporte, and finished 15th at the 1995 Worlds with Allison Gaylor.

Then Jamie and David got together, and it was magical from the beginning. Only a year after forming their partnership, they beat Elena and Anton, the reigning World champions, at Skate America. That event ushered in three seasons of brilliant competition between the two pairs.

Their athleticism allows Jamie and David to do difficult, often dangerous lifts and dismounts. And the chemistry that they have between them cannot be taught. Their signature program is "Love Story," which is appropriate because they are a couple off the ice as well.

Achievements: Olympic gold medalists, 2002; World champions, 2001; Grand Prix Final champions, 2001, 2002; Four Continents champions, 2000, 2001; three-time Canadian champions.

Elena Berezhnaya & Anton Sikharulidze

BORN (Elena)	October 1, 1977, Stavropolski, Russia
BORN (Anton)	October 25, 1976, Leningrad, Russia
HOMETOWN	St. Petersburg, Russia
COACH	Tamara Moskvina

When you have the steepest hill to climb, you appreciate reaching the top.

There was a time when it looked like Elena might never skate again, or even talk again. In January 1996, she and her former partner were skating at a rink in Riga, Latvia, when something went wrong with their side-by-side camel spins. Her partner's skate hit Elena's head and stuck there. She spent several weeks in the hospital. It took her months to get her strength and speech back.

Anton, who had trained at the same rink in St. Petersburg as Elena, came to Latvia and took her back to Russia. Soon they formed a new pairs partnership.

Within 16 months, they won the important Grand Prix Final. They might have won the gold medal at the 1998 Olympics, but they had a horrible fall on their star lift. They did win the silver, and the next month won their first World championship. After they won Worlds again in 1999, their coach moved from Russia to New Jersey. Elena and Anton followed her.

They missed their families, and it was a very difficult time. Eventually, Elena and Anton were skating as well as they ever had. Then, one day in 2000, Elena was given a prescription for cough syrup. It contained ingredients that were not permitted by officials, and she had to withdraw from Worlds.

Elena and Anton won the World silver medal in 2001, in a very close battle with Jamie Salé and David Pelletier.

That set the stage for Salt Lake City. Elena and Anton won the short program with a brilliant performance and skated a poetic freeskate. When the marks came up, Elena and Anton had beaten Jamie and David five judges to four. They were awarded the gold medals.

But later in the week it was discovered that the French judge had broken a rule, so her vote was not allowed to count. She had voted for Elena and Anton, so David and Jamie now had the same number of first-place votes. A second set of gold medals was made for them.

Elena and Anton were so welcoming of Jamie and David as co-winners that everyone felt good about the final result.

As Anton said, "It's cool the way it is."

QUICK FACTS:

- When Elena and Anton were forced to miss the 2000 World championships, Anton's old partner, Maria Petrova, won the gold with Alexei Tikhonov.

- After Jamie and David were awarded their Olympic gold medals, Anton said, "No one has asked us to cut off a piece of our well-earned medal and give it away. We are two great pairs, from two great countries, who gave two great performances."

- Jamie Salé says, "Elena and Anton have such wonderful lines. I just love watching them skate."

Achievements: Olympic gold medalists, 2002; Olympic silver medalists, 1998; World champions, 1998, 1999; World silver medalists, 2001; Grand Prix Final champions, 1998; Grand Prix Final silver medalists, 2001, 2002; European champions, 1998, 2001, 2002; four-time Russian champions.

Kyoko Ina & John Zimmerman

BORN (Kyoko)	October 11, 1972, Tokyo, Japan
BORN (John)	November 26, 1973, Birmingham, Alabama
HOMETOWNS	New York City; Birmingham
COACH	Tamara Moskvina

QUICK FACTS:

- Kyoko's mother was an Asian Games champion in swimming. Her grandmother competed at Wimbledon in tennis, and her grandfather represented Japan in track at the 1924 Summer Olympics.

- John's role model has been Artur Dmitriev, who trains at the same rink and who won Olympic championships with two different partners. The trademark spin that John and Kyoko perfected was first done by Artur and Natalia Mishkutenok.

John Zimmerman describes his pairs partnership with Kyoko Ina this way: "We are two different people and two different skaters. She is the technician and I am the artist. It has taken a while to come together."

But the duo is showing the consistency and the chemistry necessary to be among the world's elite. In the 2001–02 season, they won their third straight American title, won silver medals in all three of their Grand Prix events, finished a strong fifth at the Winter Olympics, and capped the year by finishing third at the World championships.

As their coach, the legendary Tamara Moskvina, explains, "They are no longer two individuals showing themselves, but a pair team."

John grew up in Alabama, where he learned to skate at a tiny rink in a shopping mall. He eventually formed a pairs partnership with Stephanie Stiegler, finishing third at the U.S. championships and rising as high as 15th in the world. That partnership broke up when Stephanie was injured in 1997.

Kyoko grew up in New York, but because her parents were from Japan she represented that country in junior singles. She returned to the United States and won the American junior ladies' title in 1989 before concentrating on pairs with Jason Dungjen. They won two American titles and finished fourth at the 1998 Winter Olympics at Nagano. The team broke up after those Olympics, and Kyoko and John formed a duo later that year.

"At first, it was a total mismatch," John says. They struggled with their unison, and there were falls on the throws. But with Tamara providing direction, Kyoko supplying discipline and John adding spontaneity, they worked until they had a breakthrough season – just in time for the 2002 Winter Olympics.

At Salt Lake City, John and Kyoko gave the crowd goose bumps. When they finished with their trademark spin, the applause was deafening. And – their coach promises – they will just keep getting better.

Achievements: World bronze medalists, 2002; 5th, Winter Olympics 2002; 4th, Grand Prix Final 2002; 7th, World championships 2000, 2001; 2nd, Four Continents 2000; 3rd, Four Continents 2001; three-time U.S. champions.

Shae-Lynn Bourne & Victor Kraatz

BORN (Shae-Lynn)	January 24, 1976, Chatham, Ontario
BORN (Victor)	April 7, 1971, Berlin, Germany
HOMETOWNS	Chatham, Ontario; Vancouver, British Columbia
COACH	Tatiana Tarasova

QUICK FACTS:

- Shae-Lynn and Victor have won 31 medals at international events.
- Shae-Lynn skated most of the 1999–2000 season, despite severe and painful knee damage that eventually required surgery.
- Victor speaks four languages fluently: English, Italian, German and French.

Although they did not win an Olympic medal, Shae-Lynn Bourne and Victor Kraatz have had an Olympian effect on their sport.

They have won nine Canadian ice dancing titles, more than any other couple. They were second at the 2002 Worlds, the best North American finish in 27 years. They invented hydro-blading, a gravity-defying low-to-the-ice skating technique.

And they were partly responsible for important changes in ice dance judging. When they finished fourth at the 1998 Olympics, where many thought they should have won a medal, new rules were brought in.

Shae-Lynn was originally a pairs skater. Victor, born in Germany and raised in Switzerland, won the Swiss junior ice dancing championship before his family moved to Canada in 1987.

In 1991, Victor was searching for a partner when he had a practice session with a 16 year old who was brand new to ice dancing. "Five minutes later, Shae-Lynn and I decided to try it," he recalls.

They won the Canadian junior title in their first season and then began their string of senior titles. In 1996, they won their first of four straight bronze medals at Worlds.

But their fortunes began to slide a year after their disappointment at the 1998 Olympics, and in January 2000 the couple thought about retiring. Instead they went to a new coach, who improved their technique.

They won the 2001 Grand Prix Final. At Canadian Nationals a few weeks later they received perfect 6.0s for presentation from all nine judges in the original dance, and from six of the nine for their Michael Jackson freeskate.

At the Olympics, their rapid, difficult freedance received a thundering ovation. But just as their music ended, they had a fluke accident and tumbled to the ice. They finished fourth again, but rebounded to win silver at Worlds.

"We want to thank everyone who has stuck by us," Shae-Lynn said afterward.

But it's Shae-Lynn and Victor who should be thanked for what they've done for ice dancing in North America.

Achievements: 4th, Winter Olympics 1998, 2002; World silver medalists, 2002; World bronze medalists, 1996, 1997, 1998, 1999; Grand Prix Final champions, 1997, 2002; Four Continents champions, 1999, 2001; nine-time Canadian champions.

Marina Anissina & Gwendal Peizerat

BORN (Marina)	August 8, 1975, Moscow
BORN (Gwendal)	April 21, 1972, Bron, France
HOMETOWNS	Moscow; Lyon, France
COACH	Muriel Boucher-Zazoui

Skating fans have come to expect the unexpected from Marina Anissina and Gwendal Peizerat.

How else could you describe a dance team in which *she* lifts *him* almost as often as he lifts her?

How else could you describe a dance team in which she spoke one language, he spoke another and they had to communicate in a third?

Marina was born in Russia and Gwendal in France. They originally skated with other partners, often competing against each other.

But in 1992, Marina's partner fell in love with another ice dancer and left Marina so he could skate with her. Marina couldn't find a new partner in Russia, so she sent letters to several skaters around the world. One letter was mailed to Gwendal. When Gwendal's partner retired, he and Marina teamed up to represent France, where there were better training facilities.

Since neither spoke the other's language at first, they used English to get their skating ideas across to each other. There were other differences besides language. Marina has an explosive temperament, while Gwendal is a cooler personality. But with her flaming red hair and passionate skating, and his elegance and flowing dirty-blond locks, they make a striking couple.

Soon they started experimenting with dramatic choreography and began inventing new dancing moves.

Their hard work began to pay off. In 1998, they won a bronze medal at the Olympics and in 2000, right in Nice France, they won their first World championship. They got a wild standing ovation, plus perfect 6.0s from four judges. Many people said it was the greatest night in French skating history.

They had a greater night on February 18, 2002, when they won the Olympic championship at Salt Lake City. "It's such a wonderful feeling," Gwendal says. "We've been together a long time, so this means a lot to us."

Marina and Gwendal are now professionals and will spend much of their time touring Europe.

Achievements: Olympic champions, 2002; Olympic bronze medalists, 1998; World champions, 2000; World silver medalists, 1998, 1999, 2001; European champions, 2000, 2002; Grand Prix Final champions, 2000; five-time French champions.

Naomi Lang & Peter Tchernyshev

BORN (Naomi)	December 18, 1978, Arcata, California
BORN (Peter)	February 6, 1971, St. Petersburg, Russia
HOMETOWNS	Allegan, Michigan; Waterford, Michigan
COACH	Alexander Zhulin

Naomi Lang and Peter Tchernyshev know they have to be patient. But that's something they're good at, because the road to their ice dance partnership was full of twists and turns.

"We know we're as strong as the top five teams," Peter said after he and Naomi finished 11th in ice dance at the 2002 Winter Olympics. "We have to wait our turn. It's painful sometimes, but we're going to stick it out."

In ice dancing, even the very best teams have to work their way slowly toward the top. Naomi and Peter also had to work their way toward each other.

Naomi took ballet lessons and was talented enough to dance with the Grand Rapids Ballet Company in Michigan. When she was eight years old, she saw an Ice Capades performance and decided she wanted to try figure skating, too.

Peter was born in Russia and was a singles skater until he was 18 years old, when injuries made it difficult for him to land the big jumps. He switched to ice dancing, then moved to the United States in 1992. Four years later, at the 1996 U.S. Nationals, he noticed Naomi at the junior ice dance competition. He suggested they form a team. Despite the nearly eight-year age difference, the partnership worked.

They won their first U.S. championship in 1999 and finished 10th in the world that year. In January 2001, Peter became a U.S. citizen, which meant that he and Naomi were eligible for the Olympics.

Because of her father's heritage, Naomi is a member of the Karuk Tribe in California. In February 2002, she became the first Native American to participate in a Winter Olympics. "I want to give other Native American children hope that they can make something of themselves," she said.

Most skating people believe that Peter and Naomi will be moving up in the ranks. They have flair and technical skill, and they bring a unique blend of Russian and American history to their partnership.

Achievements: 11th, Winter Olympics 2002; Four Continents champions, 2000; 8th, World championships 2000; 9th, World championships 2001, 2002; 10th, World championships 1999; four-time U.S. champions.